A LIFEGUIDE® BIBLE STUDY

M A R Y
The Lord's Servant

12 Studies
for individuals or groups

Douglas & Karen Connelly

With Notes for Leaders

InterVarsity Press
Downers Grove, Illinois

InterVarsity Press® is the book-publishing division of InterVarsity Christian Fellowship®, a student movement active on campus at hundreds of universities, colleges and schools of nursing in the United States of America, and a member movement of the International Fellowship of Evangelical Students. For information about local and regional activities, write Public Relations Dept., InterVarsity Christian Fellowship, 6400 Schroeder Rd., P.O. Box 7895, Madison, WI 53707-7895.

Cover photograph: H. Reinhard

ISBN 0-8308-1078-1

Printed in the United States of America ∞

20	19	18	17	16	15	14	13	12	11	10	09	08	07	06	05	04	03	02	01
14	13	12	11	10	09	08	07	06	05	04	03	02	01	00	99	98	97	96	

Contents

Getting the Most from LifeGuide® Bible Studies

Many of us long to fill our minds and our lives with Scripture. We desire to be transformed by its message. LifeGuide® Bible Studies are designed to be an exciting and challenging way to do just that. They help us to be guided by God's Word in every area of life.

How They Work

LifeGuides have a number of distinctive features. Perhaps the most important is that they are *inductive* rather than *deductive*. In other words, they lead us to *discover* what the Bible says rather than simply *telling* us what it says.

They are also thought-provoking. They help us to think about the meaning of the passage so that we can truly understand what the author is saying. The questions require more than one-word answers.

The studies are personal. Questions expose us to the promises, assurances, exhortations and challenges of God's Word. They are designed to allow the Scriptures to renew our minds so that we can be transformed by the Spirit of God. This is the ultimate goal of all Bible study.

The studies are versatile. They are designed for student, neighborhood and church groups. They are also effective for individual study.

How They're Put Together

LifeGuides also have a distinctive format. Each study need take no more than forty-five minutes in a group setting or thirty minutes in personal study—unless you choose to take more time.

The studies can be used within a quarter system in a church and fit well in a semester or trimester system on a college campus. If a guide has more than thirteen studies, it is divided into two or occasionally three parts of approximately twelve studies each.

LifeGuides use a workbook format. Space is provided for writing answers to each question. This is ideal for personal study and allows group members to prepare in advance for the discussion.

The studies also contain leader's notes. They show how to lead a group discussion, provide additional background information on certain questions, give helpful tips on group dynamics and suggest ways to deal with problems which may arise during the discussion. With such helps, someone with little or no experience can lead an effective study.

Suggestions for Individual Study

1. As you begin each study, pray that God will help you to understand and apply the passage to your life.

2. Read and reread the assigned Bible passage to familiarize yourself with what the author is saying. In the case of book studies, you may want to read through the entire book prior to the first study. This will give you a helpful overview of its contents.

3. A good modern translation of the Bible, rather than the King James Version or a paraphrase, will give you the most help. The New International Version, the New American Standard Bible and the Revised Standard Version are all recommended. However, the questions in this guide are based on the New International Version.

4. Write your answers in the space provided in the study guide. This will help you to express your understanding of the passage clearly.

5. It might be good to have a Bible dictionary handy. Use it to look up any unfamiliar words, names or places.

Suggestions for Group Study

1. Come to the study prepared. Follow the suggestions for individual

study mentioned above. You will find that careful preparation will greatly enrich your time spent in group discussion.

2. Be willing to participate in the discussion. The leader of your group will not be lecturing. Instead, he or she will be encouraging the members of the group to discuss what they have learned from the passage. The leader will be asking the questions that are found in this guide. Plan to share what God has taught you in your individual study.

3. Stick to the passage being studied. Your answers should be based on the verses which are the focus of the discussion and not on outside authorities such as commentaries or speakers. This guide deliberately avoids jumping from book to book or passage to passage. Each study focuses on only one passage. Book studies are generally designed to lead you through the book in the order in which it was written. This will help you follow the author's argument.

4. Be sensitive to the other members of the group. Listen attentively when they share what they have learned. You may be surprised by their insights! Link what you say to the comments of others so the group stays on the topic. Also, be affirming whenever you can. This will encourage some of the more hesitant members of the group to participate.

5. Be careful not to dominate the discussion. We are sometimes so eager to share what we have learned that we leave too little opportunity for others to respond. By all means participate! But allow others to also.

6. Expect God to teach you through the passage being discussed and through the other members of the group. Pray that you will have an enjoyable and profitable time together.

7. If you are the discussion leader, you will find additional suggestions and helpful ideas for each study in the leader's notes. These are found at the back of the guide.

Introducing Mary

Mary, the mother of Jesus, is one of the most intriguing people to fill the pages of Scripture. She is also one of the most neglected and misunderstood. Some Christians revere Mary deeply, but know very little about what the Bible says about her. Other Christians (perhaps in reaction to those who exalt Mary too highly) almost ignore her. For many of us Mary has become little more than a plastic figure in our Christmas nativity scenes. After the holiday season, she is dusted off and put away for another year.

The biblical record presents Mary as a woman of extraordinary character. She was humble and obedient to God and yet was a woman of incredible strength. She loved the Lord God of Israel with all her heart and mind, and she learned what it was like to trust him completely. Mary was "graced" by God above all other women. She was the channel through which God the Son became human.

But Mary was used of God on a much larger canvas than the stable of Bethlehem. Mary nurtured and trained Jesus through the years of his childhood and adolescence. She worried about a son she thought was working too hard against too much opposition. She stood at the cross watching her own child die a torturous death. In fact, Mary was the only human being present at both the birth and death of Jesus. The privilege she was given by God's grace carried a heavy price.

Our focus in this study guide is on what the Bible says about Mary and what we can learn from Mary's example. We have come to this study of Mary as a man and a woman who desire like Mary to be obedient to the Lord, and we've been deeply challenged about the shallowness of our commitment. As Christian parents who want to cultivate godliness and devotion in our children, we've learned from Mary. We have looked at Mary as believers who want to be blessed in our walk with the Lord. What we have found in Mary is more than a cold mosaic staring at us from a church wall. We have discovered a woman who heard God's call upon her life and responded faithfully.

We want you to walk the pathway of Mary's life with us. Let her life choices challenge you. Learn her obedient ways. We know you won't be the same at the end of the study. God is searching today, just as he did two thousand years ago, for women and men of strength and godly character—genuine servants of the Lord.

1
Nothing Is Impossible
Luke 1:26-38

Karen's grandmother was a remarkable woman. Luda Bishop was married at fifteen, just two years after her own mother died. Luda's five-year-old brother went with her to her new husband's home. The man she married was a twenty-eight-year-old widower who had two sons of his own—a nine-year-old and a five-year-old. Luda took on the responsibility of marriage, a household and three children as a teenager!

The woman God chose when he sent an angel to a tiny town in Galilee was probably not much older than Luda Bishop. After a brief encounter with this startling messenger, Mary's life changed forever.

---

1. Describe a time in your experience, or in the experience of someone you know, when your whole life's direction was changed by one event or decision.

2. Read Luke 1:26-38. This passage chronicles some amazing events. What words and phrases give you an idea of what this experience was like for Mary?

---

3. The angel referred to Mary twice as "favored" by God (vv. 28, 30). The word is based on the Greek word for grace. What insight does that give you into why God chose Mary to give birth to Jesus?

---

4. What does the fact that Mary was "greatly troubled" (v. 29) by the angel's greeting reveal about Mary's spiritual self-image?

---

5. What specific information does the angel Gabriel give to Mary about the son she would bear (vv. 31-33, 35)?

---

6. Mary responds to the angel's declaration by asking how the promise would be fulfilled (v. 34). Do you think Mary's question was an expression of doubt? Explain.

---

7. What do you think would have been your response to a call from God for such a sacrifice on your part?

8. The angel tells Mary that her relative Elizabeth has conceived (v. 36). What effect would that information have on Mary?

---

9. After the angel disappeared, what thoughts and feelings must have come upon Mary as she thought about Joseph?

as she thought about her family?

as she thought about her own reputation and future?

---

10. In what area of your life do you need to believe that "nothing is impossible with God" (v. 37)?

What keeps you from fully trusting God in that area?

2
Strength to Obey

Luke 1:39-56

Several years ago we went through a very difficult time in our lives. Failure, loss, rejection and pain were feelings we wrestled with every day. In those dark days, God gave us a few courageous Christians who determined to love us through the storm that was breaking over our lives. Sometimes their love was expressed in a simple hug or prayer. Sometimes they insisted we get out of the house and enjoy an ice cream cone with them. At other times they were just willing to cry with us.

It is significant that, after the angel Gabriel left, Mary went to visit her relative, Elizabeth. Mary knew that Elizabeth would give her emotional support and spiritual counsel. When the thrill of saying yes to God passes, and we are in the hard place of obedience to God, we need spiritual friends to help us through.

1. Recall a time when another believer encouraged you. In what practical ways did that person minister to you?

2. Read Luke 1:39-45. What did the Holy Spirit reveal to Elizabeth about Mary?

---

3. What did the Spirit reveal to Elizabeth about her own baby's leap in her womb?

---

4. In what way would the information given by God to Elizabeth encourage Mary and strengthen her faith?

---

5. Read Luke 1:46-56. What aspects of God's character are mentioned in Mary's praise to God?

---

6. Which of these attributes of God is most reflected in your life?

Which is reflected least?

---

7. How does Mary describe herself in her poem to God?

8. In verse 47 Mary refers to the Lord as "God my *Savior.*" What does that phrase tell you about Mary's perception of her own spiritual need?

---

9. In this passage we've seen Mary's faith in God, her humble servantlike attitude, and her personal knowledge of the character of God. Which of these traits is most lacking in your life?

What specific steps can you take to cultivate that trait?

---

10. Since the earliest days of the church, Mary's words have been sung as a hymn of worship to God. Based on this passage, what should characterize the content and spirit of our songs of praise and worship?

---

11. As you reflect on God's goodness to you, you may want to write a song or poem or letter to God that expresses your joy in him. Then pray or sing or read what you have written. Share your "hymn" with your group or with a Christian friend.

3
Divine Interruption
Matthew 1:18-25

On Tuesday, November 8, 1994, the minivan carrying Scott and Janet Willis and six of their children hit a piece of steel that had fallen on a Milwaukee expressway. The steel punctured the gas tank, and the vehicle burst into flames. Scott and Janet and one child tumbled from the car. They rolled in the median grass to extinguish their burning clothes. As they rushed back to their van, they saw to their horror that it was engulfed in flames. Five children perished immediately; the sixth child died the next day.

At a televised news conference two days later, Scott and Janet gave powerful and eloquent testimony to the grace of God in their lives. With bandaged hands and broken hearts, they told a watching nation about their confident trust in the goodness of God even in the face of what we consider a tragedy. In the middle of a tragic interruption in their lives, two believers made a choice to cling to God alone for comfort and security.

The man engaged to Mary found his life interrupted too. When Joseph learned that Mary was pregnant, he thought he had only two options—to publicly disgrace the woman he loved or to end their relationship in a private divorce. God's intervention, however, opened up a whole new option that he had never considered.

1. How do you normally respond to life's interruptions?

_____

2. Read Matthew 1:18-25. What feelings would you struggle with if you were Joseph?

_____

3. What does Joseph's decision in verse 19 tell you about what kind of man he was?

_____

4. Why do you think God let Joseph work through the struggle of that difficult decision before revealing the true story of Mary's child to him?

_____

5. How do you think a typical church might have handled this situation?

_____

6. How did Joseph know that this was a genuine encounter with an angel and not a case of wishful thinking on his part?

7. What confirmation about Mary's character do you find in this passage?

8. What do you think Joseph said to his family after his encounter with the angel?

9. What specific truths can you learn about who Jesus was and what he came to do from the angel's words (vv. 20-21) and from Matthew's reference to Old Testament prophecy (vv. 22-23)?

10. What qualities do you see demonstrated in Joseph's life that would have equipped him to be a good husband to Mary and a godly model to Jesus?

11. What principles can you learn from this passage that will prepare you for the next divine interruption in your own life?

4
Strange Blessings
Luke 2:1-20

We are second-time-around parents. We have two adult children—and a five-year-old! When we first learned that Karen was pregnant with Kyle it seemed like the timing was all wrong. We were in a period of painful transition in our lives. We had planned on Karen's working full time to help out financially. We didn't want to be parents of a newborn at forty years old! In spite of our confusion, however, God was working out his perfect will. The Lord met every need during that difficult time—and gave us a child who brings joy to our lives every day.

Mary knew that the child she was carrying was God's Son, but that didn't change her situation or make the trip to Bethlehem shorter. We've made the story of Jesus' birth warm and fuzzy, when in fact the setting was dreadful. Mary gave birth to Jesus without help from any family members or a midwife. Her only assistance came from a faithful husband—and an unfailing God.

1. Have you ever had to face a difficult time in your life alone? Describe that situation and what feelings you struggled with.

2. Read Luke 2:1-7. What different events came together to bring Mary and Joseph to this place at this time?

3. What doubts about God's wisdom and timing might have accompanied Mary on the journey to Bethlehem?

4. Describe the scene in the stable as you think it really was. Include both positive and negative aspects.

5. What principles from Mary's song (see especially Luke 1:50-53) are demonstrated in Mary's situation?

6. What impresses you most about Joseph and Mary in this story?

7. Read Luke 2:8-20. Describe the setting for the announcement of the good news (who was involved, where, when and why).

What does this tell you about how God's direction may come to you?

_____

8. Mary was sharing a very intimate personal experience with strangers. What does her response (v. 19) tell you about her?

_____

9. In what practical ways can you begin to record and remember instances of God's blessing and guidance in your life?

_____

10. The shepherds spread the word to others (vv. 17-18, 20). What does that tell you about what they experienced?

_____

11. What good news about Jesus' blessings in your life would you like to tell someone else about?

5
The Day After Christmas

Luke 2:21-40

Do you ever feel like a minor character in the great drama of life? Maybe a stage hand, a set designer or the character who never speaks a line. You may wonder what significance your role has in God's eyes.

Most people are very familiar with the main characters in the Christmas story. However, we aren't nearly as familiar with what happened in the weeks *after* Jesus was born. We usually skip over the people who have a minor part to play.

Some actors in the divine drama may seem like unimportant characters to us, but they certainly weren't unimportant to God. In fact, from God's perspective the real minor characters in this story were people like Caesar Augustus. He grabbed the headlines in his day but received only passing reference in Scripture. Two aged people sweep past us in this passage in Luke's Gospel, but they were used by God to bring encouragement and insight into Mary's life.

1. Describe an older person who has made a positive impact on you (perhaps someone who would have been overlooked by others). What qualities of that person's character do you remember most?

2. Read Luke 2:21-40. In what ways did Mary and Joseph fulfill God's Law?

What was the importance of each of their actions?

3. What does this obedience reveal about Mary and Joseph's devotion to the Lord?

4. What do Mary and Joseph's actions show about the influence of a parent on a very young child?

5. What specific ministries did the Holy Spirit perform in Simeon's life (vv. 25-35)?

6. What do Simeon's two prophecies (vv. 29-35) reveal about Jesus' future?

about Mary's future?

about Simeon's own future?

---

7. Put yourself in Mary and Joseph's place. You have just heard startling predictions about your child. Then a prophetess comes and adds her own praise and revelations (vv. 36-38). How do you think Simeon and Anna affected them?

---

8. What results would their predictions produce in Jesus' parents as they returned home?

---

9. What impact do you want to have on people as you grow older?

What are you doing to cultivate that influence now?

---

10. Who could you encourage about the importance of their role in God's work? Plan a specific way to bring your encouragement to that person.

6
Spiritual Mentoring
Luke 2:41-52

Awindow washer came to clean the large windows in our church building a few weeks ago. He brought along his young son as his helper. The little boy was extremely perceptive, and he kept pummeling his father with difficult questions—questions about his equipment, questions about the church furniture, questions about how glass is made. The father found himself more and more frustrated and finally said through clenched teeth, "Son, I don't know the answers to all these questions. Find something to do!"

If we as parents get frustrated at times with our children, imagine being given the responsibility of parenting God's Son. Mary and Joseph must have found that task incredibly challenging.

1. What was most challenging for your parents about raising you?

2. Read Luke 2:41-52. What events in this passage would be difficult for a parent to deal with?

3. What does Mary and Joseph's obedience to God's command to come to Jerusalem for the Passover tell you about their personal and family life?

4. Were Mary and Joseph wrong to travel a full day's journey before they began looking for Jesus? Explain your answer.

5. How would you describe Mary and Joseph's reaction to Jesus?

Was it justified or not?

6. How would you characterize Jesus' response to his parents (v. 49)?

7. Jesus saw his fellowship with other believers and his participation in corporate worship as a fulfillment of his Father's business. How would your worship experience be different if you viewed it as a visit to your Father's house?

8. By this point in his life, Jesus had become aware of his unique calling to be God's Messiah. Through what means had Jesus come to that understanding of who he was and what he would do?

9. In light of all they had been told since before Jesus' conception, why didn't Mary and Joseph understand Jesus' mission?

10. In what other ways might Jesus have felt the tension between obedience to his Father and obedience to Mary and Joseph as he grew into manhood?

11. Notice Mary's response in verse 51. What does this passage reveal about her character as a parent?

12. Whether or not you are a parent, what can you learn about managing your responsibilities to others and to God from this passage?

7
Letting Go
John 2:1-11

Our daughter, Kimberly, became engaged a few months ago—and it was interesting to watch the transition. Her loyalties began to move gradually from us to Mike, her fiancé. Decisions and problems are discussed with Mike before they are mentioned to us. If something hilarious happens at work, Kim bypasses us to share the laughter on the phone first with Mike. We are glad to see those new bonds forming, but it means the old parental bonds have to change.

Launching a child into adulthood is a threatening experience for some parents. For others it is a time of joy as they see their children leave the nest to fly on their own. Jesus grew into manhood as a loving, supportive son, but the day came when Jesus had to follow the voice of his heavenly Father alone.

---

1. What was the most difficult tie to break with your parents as you grew into adulthood?

2. Read John 2:1-11. What impresses you about Jesus' relationship with Mary?

_____

3. What do you think Mary expected Jesus to do about the lack of wine? (Remember, according to verse 11, Jesus had not performed any miracles before this.)

_____

4. Jesus' response to Mary in verse 4 could be paraphrased: "What does this problem of *yours* have to do with *me?*" Why does he respond in this way?

_____

5. Mary's words in verse 5 are the last direct words of Mary recorded in the New Testament. What do they reveal about her relationship with Jesus?

_____

6. What insight does verse 11 give you on why Jesus chose to perform this miracle?

_____

7. What did the disciples gain from observing the miracle?

8. Do you think Mary was surprised at how Jesus handled the situation? Explain why or why not.

9. How did this incident change the relationship between Jesus and Mary?

10. What situation or relationship in your life would you like to see change?

If Jesus was willing to change that situation or relationship with a dramatic miracle or through a process that involves your obedience and faith, which method would you prefer and why?

11. What steps toward change can you make whether the dramatic miracle comes or not?

8
Family & Faith

Mark 3:13-21, 31-35

The woman sitting in Doug's office was sobbing so hard she could barely speak. "It's my son," she finally managed to say. "He's made an awful decision."

Doug's mind was racing while she spoke. He knew her son to be a very serious, committed Christian. He had just attended an Urbana conference with a dozen other college students from our church. He couldn't imagine what the son had done to devastate his mother—but certainly wasn't prepared for what she said.

"He has signed up for a missions training program. He wants to go to some primitive place and share the gospel. I can't believe he would throw away four years of college to do *that!*"

The young man's mother left Doug's office without much comfort from him. Doug told her that he admired her son's courage and sacrificial commitment. He encouraged her to pray for her son and for God's peace in her own heart.

Sometimes those we love the most become the biggest roadblocks to our pursuit of the will of God. Even Jesus had to deal with a mother who wondered if he was pushing too hard.

1. Describe a conflict that has arisen between you and a family member over a spiritual issue. How was that conflict resolved?

2. Read Mark 3:13-21. Compare and contrast how Jesus must have felt as he selected his apostles (vv. 13-19) and as he found himself immersed in ministry (vv. 20-21).

3. What can you see in this passage that would make Jesus' family conclude that Jesus was "out of his mind"?

4. What kind of family discussions might Jesus' family members have had before deciding to intervene?

5. What do you think they intended to do with Jesus (v. 21)?

6. Read Mark 3:31-35. Describe the tone of Jesus' reaction to his family's request.

7. How has your commitment to Christ affected your relationship with your family?

8. What can we learn from Jesus' example about our relationship to our human family compared with our submission to Christ's lordship?

_____

9. In light of Jesus' statement in verse 35, how should Christians relate to each other?

_____

10. It seems surprising that Mary would have tried to hinder Jesus in view of all the things she had been told about her son and his mission in the world. What do you think might have motivated Mary to come to Jesus on this occasion?

_____

11. Describe a time in your experience or in the experience of someone you know when a fellow Christian stepped forward in the role of a parent or brother or sister and ministered to you.

_____

12. What could you do or say this week that would help your family better understand your faith in and commitment to Christ as Lord?

_____

What fellow Christian can you ask to pray with you and to hold you accountable to take that practical step of witness to your family?

9
Standing Near the Cross

John 19:23-30

We have never had to experience what many Christian parents have had to endure—the death of one of our children. However, we've walked through that valley of grief with other people, and we've tasted the bitter tears of their sorrow.

One truth we have often shared with grieving parents is that our heavenly Father knows what it is like to have a child die. Above the cross on which Jesus suffered, the Father watched with a broken heart. What we don't often realize is that Jesus' mother, Mary, was watching too. As she stood near the cross, she realized what Simeon had meant thirty-three years earlier when he told her that a sword would pierce her own heart.

---

1. What important event have you witnessed either in person or through television? What were your thoughts and feelings as you watched?

2. Read John 19:23-30. Contrast the attitudes and actions of the soldiers in verses 23-24 with the attitude and actions of Jesus in verses 26-27.

_____

3. What does Jesus' expression of concern for his mother at this crucial moment in his life tell you about his relationship with her?

_____

4. Do you think Mary wondered if her obedience to God's call had been worth it as she watched Jesus die? Explain.

_____

5. How would you have felt as a follower of Jesus as you stood near his cross?

_____

6. Why do you think Jesus chose to entrust the care of his mother to the "disciple whom he loved"?

_____

7. What practical ministry can you have this week to a Christian in need?

8. What aspects of this account of the crucifixion are tragic and unjust?

What aspects are triumphant?

9. Do you think Mary understood why Jesus had to die in this way? Explain.

10. How would you explain the necessity of Jesus' death on the cross to another person?

11. In what ways can you thank Christ for his sacrifice on the cross for you?

10
Our Spiritual Legacy
Acts 1:12-14; 2:1-4

Doug meets twice a month with Tom Skaff and Steve Aikman for breakfast. They meet for more than just a meal, however. They meet to hold each other accountable to live godly lives. Earlier this year, they were challenged to think about what they want the significant people in their lives to say about them at their funerals! At first it sounded pretty morbid, but the longer they thought about the legacy they wanted to leave behind, the more they were motivated to cultivate Christlike qualities in their lives right now.

We catch our final glimpses of Mary in the New Testament as she identifies herself with the early church. Her lingering legacy is her ministry to that small band of people who had committed themselves to Jesus as Savior and Lord. Mary takes her place not apart from other Christians and not above them either. She takes her place in fellowship with those who were followers of her own son.

1. What do you want people to say about you when your life ends? (Consider family, Christian friends, business associates and neighbors.)

2. Read Acts 1:12-14, which directly follows the ascension of Christ. Describe the setting for and participants in this gathering.

3. Earlier in his ministry Jesus' family had concluded that Jesus was out of his mind. How do you account for their change in attitude?

4. What strengths would Mary's presence have added to this group of believers?

5. What strengths or gifts do you bring to your church or study group?

6. Read Acts 2:1-4. Mary and Jesus' brothers were most likely part of this group. What words and phrases highlight the power of this event?

7. Do you think Mary and the other followers of Jesus were surprised by the events in these verses? Explain your answer.

8. How does the Spirit strengthen your spiritual life?

9. In what ways had Jesus left a spiritual legacy for Mary and the other disciples?

10. What one aspect of Mary's life experience has touched you most deeply over the course of this study?

11. What aspect of Mary's spiritual legacy would you like to make a part of your own legacy?

How can you do that?

Leader's Notes

Leading a Bible discussion can be an enjoyable and rewarding experience. But it can also be *scary*—especially if you've never done it before. If this is your feeling, you're in good company. When God asked Moses to lead the Israelites out of Egypt, he replied, "O Lord, please send someone else to do it!" (Ex 4:13).

When Solomon became king of Israel, he felt the task was beyond his abilities. "I am only a little child and do not know how to carry out my duties. . . . Who is able to govern this great people of yours?" (1 Kings 3:7, 9).

When God called Jeremiah to be a prophet, he replied, "Ah, Sovereign LORD, . . . I do not know how to speak; I am only a child" (Jer 1:6).

The list goes on. The apostles were "unschooled, ordinary men" (Acts 4:13). Timothy was young, frail and frightened. Paul's "thorn in the flesh" made him feel weak. But God's response to all of his servants—including you—is essentially the same: "My grace is sufficient for you" (2 Cor 12:9). Relax. God helped these people in spite of their weaknesses, and he can help you in spite of your feelings of inadequacy.

There is another reason why you should feel encouraged. Leading a Bible discussion is not difficult if you follow certain guidelines. You don't need to be an expert on the Bible or a trained teacher. The suggestions listed below should enable you to effectively and enjoyably fulfill your role as leader.

Preparing to Lead

1. Ask God to help you understand and apply the passage to your own life. Unless this happens, you will not be prepared to lead others. Pray too for the various members of the group. Ask God to give you an enjoyable and profitable time together studying his Word.

2. As you begin each study, read and reread the assigned Bible passage to familiarize yourself with what the author is saying. In the case of book studies, you may want to read through the entire book prior to the first study. This will give you a helpful overview of its contents.

3. This study guide is based on the New International Version of the Bible. It will help you and the group if you use this translation as the basis for your study and discussion. Encourage others to use the NIV also, but allow them the freedom to use whatever translation they prefer.

4. Carefully work through each question in the study. Spend time in meditation and reflection as you formulate your answers.

5. Write your answers in the space provided in the study guide. This will help you to express your understanding of the passage clearly.

6. It might help you to have a Bible dictionary handy. Use it to look up any unfamiliar words, names or places. (For additional help on how to study a passage, see chapter five of *Leading Bible Discussions,* IVP.)

7. Once you have finished your own study of the passage, familiarize yourself with the leader's notes for the study you are leading. These are designed to help you in several ways. First, they tell you the purpose the study guide author had in mind while writing the study. Take time to think through how the study questions work together to accomplish that purpose. Second, the notes provide you with additional background information or comments on some of the questions. This information can be useful if people have difficulty understanding or answering a question. Third, the leader's notes can alert you to potential problems you may encounter during the study.

8. If you wish to remind yourself of anything mentioned in the leader's notes, make a note to yourself below that question in the study.

Leading the Study

1. Begin the study on time. Unless you are leading an evangelistic Bible study, open with prayer, asking God to help you to understand and apply the passage.

2. Be sure that everyone in your group has a study guide. Encourage them to prepare beforehand for each discussion by working through the questions in the guide.

3. At the beginning of your first time together, explain that these studies are meant to be discussions not lectures. Encourage the members of the group to participate. However, do not put pressure on those who may be hesitant to speak during the first few sessions.

4. Read the introductory paragraph at the beginning of the discussion. This will orient the group to the passage being studied.

5. Read the passage aloud if you are studying one chapter or less. You may choose to do this yourself, or someone else may read if he or she has been asked to do so prior to the study. Longer passages may occasionally be read in parts at different times during the study. Some studies may cover several chapters. In such cases reading aloud would probably take too much time, so the group members should simply read the assigned passages prior to the study.

6. As you begin to ask the questions in the guide, keep several things in mind. First, the questions are designed to be used just as they are written. If you wish, you may simply read them aloud to the group. Or you may prefer to express them in your own words. However, unnecessary rewording of the questions is not recommended.

Second, the questions are intended to guide the group toward understanding and applying the *main idea* of the passage. The author of the guide has stated his or her view of this central idea in the *purpose* of the study in the leader's notes. You should try to understand how the passage expresses this idea and how the study questions work together to lead the group in that direction.

There may be times when it is appropriate to deviate from the study guide. For example, a question may have already been answered. If so, move on to the next question. Or someone may raise an important question not covered in the guide. Take time to discuss it! The important thing is to use discretion. There may be many routes you can travel to reach the goal of the study. But the easiest route is usually the one the author has suggested.

7. Avoid answering your own questions. If necessary, repeat or rephrase them until they are clearly understood. An eager group quickly becomes passive and silent if they think the leader will do most of the talking.

8. Don't be afraid of silence. People may need time to think about the question before formulating their answers.

9. Don't be content with just one answer. Ask, "What do the rest of you think?" or "Anything else?" until several people have given answers to the question.

10. Acknowledge all contributions. Try to be affirming whenever possible. Never reject an answer. If it is clearly wrong, ask, "Which verse led you to that conclusion?" or again, "What do the rest of you think?"

11. Don't expect every answer to be addressed to you, even though this will probably happen at first. As group members become more at ease, they will begin to truly interact with each other. This is one sign of a healthy discussion.

12. Don't be afraid of controversy. It can be very stimulating. If you don't resolve an issue completely, don't be frustrated. Move on and keep it in mind for later. A subsequent study may solve the problem.

13. Stick to the passage under consideration. It should be the source for answering the questions. Discourage the group from unnecessary cross-referencing. Likewise, stick to the subject and avoid going off on tangents.

14. Periodically summarize what the *group* has said about the passage. This helps to draw together the various ideas mentioned and gives continuity to the study. But don't preach.

15. Conclude your time together with conversational prayer. Be sure to ask God's help to apply those things which you learned in the study.

16. End on time.

Many more suggestions and helps are found in *Leading Bible Discussions* (IVP). Reading and studying through that would be well worth your time.

Components of Small Groups

A healthy small group should do more than study the Bible. There are four components you should consider as you structure your time together.

Nurture. Being a part of a small group should be a nurturing and edifying experience. You should grow in your knowledge and love of God and each other. If we are to properly love God, we must know and keep his commandments (Jn 14:15). That is why Bible study should be a foundational part of your small group. But you can be nurtured by other things as well. You can memorize Scripture, read and discuss a book, or occasionally listen to a tape of a good speaker.

Community. Most people have a need for close friendships. Your small group can be an excellent place to cultivate such relationships. Allow time for informal interaction before and after the study. Have a time of sharing during the meeting. Do fun things together as a group, such as a potluck supper or a picnic. Have someone bring refreshments to the meeting. Be creative!

Worship. A portion of your time together can be spent in worship and prayer. Praise God together for who he is. Thank him for what he has done and is doing in your lives and in the world. Pray for each other's needs. Ask God to help you to apply what you have learned. Sing hymns together.

Mission. Many small groups decide to work together in some form of outreach. This can be a practical way of applying what you have learned. You can host a series of evangelistic discussions for your friends or neighbors. You can visit people at a home for the elderly. Help a widow with cleaning or repair jobs around her home. Such projects can have a transforming influence on your group.

For a detailed discussion of the nature and function of small groups, read *Small Group Leaders' Handbook* or *The Big Book on Small Groups* (both from IVP).

Study 1. Nothing Is Impossible. Luke 1:26-38.

Purpose: To help us see what is involved in being obedient to God's direction in our lives.

General Note. As the group leader for this Bible study, you may want to prepare by doing some reading about Mary from a biblical perspective. Unfortunately, not much has been written on Mary from an evangelical position. Much of what has been written tends to be overly sentimental. A good Bible dictionary will give you an overview of the New Testament portrait of Mary. You may also want to read some of the articles in the *Dictionary of Jesus and the Gospels* (Downers Grove, Ill.: InterVarsity Press, 1992). Jack Hayford's little book *The Mary Miracle* (Ventura, Calif.: Regal, 1994) is a good resource for practical and devotional insight.

If you have people in your group from a Roman Catholic background, you should be familiar with the basic tenets of Catholic belief about Mary. Rather than engaging in long debates over the validity of Catholic dogma about Mary, a better approach will be to keep the focus of the discussion on what we can learn from the New Testament about Mary.

Question 2. Mary is traditionally pictured as a young woman, although no direct statement is made about her age. The normal betrothal age was fourteen, although a woman as young as twelve could be betrothed. The Jewish marriage process had two stages. In the betrothal period an agreement was made (usually between the fathers) that a man and a woman would marry. Often a financial exchange was also made as the bride's father paid the bride price or dowry to the groom or the groom's father. At this point the man and woman were legally betrothed. A divorce was required to break the agreement. The betrothal normally lasted one year, and it was during this time that Gabriel visited Mary. The second stage of the marriage process was the actual marriage ceremony, when the husband took his wife to his home, and the marriage was consummated through sexual union.

Question 3. God's choice of Mary as the woman through whom the Messiah would be born was based on God's grace, not on any inherent quality in Mary. God had used his Spirit and his Word to prepare Mary to be receptive to God's request, but Mary's "blessed" status was a gift bestowed by God alone.

The angel Gabriel appears four times in Scripture to men and women uniquely chosen and blessed by God. He always brings a significant message of hope for the people of God. Gabriel appeared twice to Daniel (Dan 8:15-19; 9:20-27); he appeared to an old priest named Zechariah to announce the birth of John the Baptizer (Lk 1:11-20); six months later he appeared to Mary.

Question 5. The name *Jesus* is the Greek form of the Hebrew name *Joshua,* and it means "the Lord saves." The child's name summarized the whole purpose of his coming—to be our Savior. Gabriel's declaration that this child would be "the Son of the Most High" (v. 32) would have meant only one thing in Mary's Jewish mind. To say that someone was "the son" of someone else meant that the person had the same nature as the father. Mary's child would have the same inherent nature as God Most High.

Question 6. It seems that Mary believes what the angel says, but wants to know how such an event can occur. We have Mary's testimony before an angel of God that she is a virgin. Gabriel does not tell Mary specifically how she will conceive; he simply declares that God will do it! Our confidence in the fact of Jesus' conception in a virgin woman rests on the trustworthiness of the Scriptural record and the awesome ability of God to do what he promises to do. No "biological" explanation is possible; it was a supernatural act of God.

Question 8. Mary must have been encouraged and strengthened in her faith to hear of another work of God's power. Elizabeth had conceived in her old age, but she had conceived through her husband, Zechariah (Lk 1:5-25). In contrast, Mary would conceive miraculously by the Holy Spirit. The fact of Elizabeth's pregnancy may have encouraged Mary, but her submission to God's will was a test of her own faith and was not based on confirming evidence.

Question 9. The angel came to Mary alone. He did not write his announcement in the sky above Nazareth. Mary would have to face the accusations and suspicions of other people all her life. Jesus himself was subtly accused by his enemies of being conceived illegitimately (Jn 8:41).

Study 2. Strength to Obey. Luke 1:39-56.

Purpose: To discover how to experience and demonstrate the joy that comes as we submit to God's will.

Question 2. The exact relationship between Mary and Elizabeth is uncertain. Elizabeth belonged to the descendants of Aaron (Lk 1:5); Mary was from the tribe of Judah and the descendants of David (Lk 1:27). The word *relative* in Luke 1:36 is a broad term covering many possible relationships. We do know that Mary and Elizabeth knew each other well.

Elizabeth was given direct knowledge from the Holy Spirit that Mary was carrying the promised Messiah. The Spirit also in some mysterious way produced a response to the unborn child Jesus in the unborn child John and then revealed to Elizabeth the spiritual significance of her baby's leap in the womb.

Question 5. Mary's words are written in poetic form like an Old Testament psalm or hymn. Verses 46-55 are sometimes referred to as the Magnificat, because in the Latin version of the Bible (called the Vulgate) the first word of the poem is the Latin word *magnificat* ("glorifies").

Mary knew the Old Testament Scriptures. This poem is a series of quotations or allusions to Old Testament passages, most of them in the Psalms. A good reference Bible will direct you to more than twenty

Scripture passages from which Mary draws her expressions of praise to God.

Mary also refers to the Lord at least eighteen times by name or with a pronoun. She sings back to God the wonderful aspects of his character that she has discovered in the Word of God and that she has learned in her personal experience.

Question 8. While Mary was chosen by God in grace to bear his Son, she also recognized her own need for God's salvation. The Roman Catholic dogma of the immaculate conception of Mary (which teaches that Mary was miraculously preserved from inheriting a sinful nature from her parents) is based on the declarations of the Catholic Church, not on Scripture. The immaculate conception of Mary was proclaimed as official Catholic dogma by Pope Pius IX in 1854.

Question 10. Our praise to God is to be based on biblical truth about God (as distinct from our opinions or "feelings" about what God is like), and it is to exalt and honor God's name and character. Those criteria apply to words of our praise music and the style of its presentation. The audience in worship is God; music and message are first of all to please him.

Question 11. This exercise provides an opportunity for creative expressions of praise to God. Depending on the talents and interests of the group, you may want to encourage instrumental music, vocal expressions, drama, poetry—whatever expressions of praise to God that come from a sincere desire to honor him.

Study 3. Divine Interruption. Matthew 1:18-25.

Purpose: To consider how we can respond appropriately to life's divine interruptions.

Question 3. Divorce was required to break the betrothal or engagement commitment. (See note for question 2 in study 1.) Because Joseph knew he was not the father of Mary's child, the only conclusion he could draw was that she had been unfaithful to him. In order to preserve his own reputation for righteousness, he knew he had to put her away. His love for Mary determined how he would do that.

The righteous standard of the Law demanded that a woman who was unfaithful during the engagement period was to be stoned along with her male counterpart (Deut 22:23-24). Jewish tradition allowed an engaged husband to divorce his promised wife. In a public divorce, the man would charge the woman openly before a religious tribunal. The woman was shamed and disgraced in front of everyone. The alternative was a private divorce carried out before two or three witnesses. Joseph wrestled with the alternatives and finally decided that he would not publicly disgrace the woman he loved so much.

Question 4. God often allows us to come to the end of our wisdom and resources before he intervenes. Just when we think we have a situation all worked out or just when we are about to collapse, God acts to prove himself compassionate and wise. This testing of our faith produces patience—the willingness to trust God fully the next time we face a difficult situation. We *are* to think through hard decisions, but only after we have asked God to give us his wisdom (Jas 1:2-6).

Question 6. Several factors converge to demonstrate that this was a genuine message from God through an angel. First, Joseph had already settled on a decision to divorce Mary. He wasn't seeking some accommodation. Second, the angel's message confirmed Mary's account that the child was supernaturally conceived. Third, the angel's message was verified by an appeal to the prophetic Scriptures (vv. 22-23). Isaiah had predicted a miraculous conception of the Messiah.

Question 7. Mary had no way of defending her purity before Joseph. Mary's character was defended to Joseph by God's declaration through an angel; her character is defended before us by the reliable record of Scripture. If Jesus was born of an immoral relationship with another man or out of an unlawful relationship with Joseph, he was not God in human flesh, and the Bible (at least at this point) is a lie. The virgin conception of Jesus is not a biblical truth that can simply be ignored; it is part of the core of the Christian faith.

Question 9. Every major strand of biblical truth about Jesus is touched by the angelic message. Jesus would be supernaturally conceived (a unique being); he would carry out a saving work; and he would be the visible presence of the invisible God—God with us.

Question 10. Not much more is said in Scripture about Joseph outside this passage. Sometimes a righteous person lives his or her whole life in relative obscurity. Joseph's quiet contribution to this marriage and home, however, laid a strong foundation for Jesus' spiritual and emotional development. We may be quietly used of God to help someone else do great things for God.

Study 4. Strange Blessings. Luke 2:1-20.
Purpose: To see in Mary's experience the sacrifice that may be required as we obey God.

Question 2. Caesar Augustus was the first and probably the most successful of all the Roman emperors. He reigned from 31 B.C. to 14 A.D. The census he ordered had two purposes: to establish records for taxation and to identify men capable of serving in the military. Six hundred and fifty years before Caesar signed the census decree, God had moved the prophet Micah to predict that the Messiah would be born in David's city of Bethlehem (Mic 5:2). In his sovereign power, God directed Caesar to issue a decree that would cause an unknown man and his pregnant wife to make a journey from Nazareth in Galilee to Bethlehem in Judea. Caesar thought *he* was in control of the empire, but he wasn't. God was the one in control.

Question 4. No one in the Bible has been attacked more unfairly than the innkeeper who sent Joseph and expectant Mary to the stable for the night. His action seems cruel and heartless until you understand what first-century inns were like. Provincial inns were simply four walls and a roof enclosing a large open area. The center of the room housed the animals of the travelers. A low platform around the perimeter provided a sleeping area for the people. There was no privacy. Instead of turning Mary and Joseph away, the innkeeper let them stay in his own private stable. Tradition says the stable was a cave. It was dry and private—but it must have been dirty and smelly!

Question 5. Mary had praised God for his compassion toward the lowly and humble. It would be difficult to imagine a setting more humble than this one. Luke (who was a physician as well as a meticulous historian) is careful to note that *Mary* gave birth to Jesus and bundled him in the long strips of cloth customarily used to wrap newborn children. At a time when Mary needed help and care as at no other time in a woman's life, she and Joseph were all alone.

Question 7. The announcement of the coming of the Messiah did not come to the political or religious leaders of the nation. The angels came to people whose hearts were open enough to believe their message. These shepherds were not on a quest for spiritual enlightenment; they were just doing their everyday jobs. God often gives us direction and insight into his will for us as we simply do what is at hand to do.

Question 8. Mary and Joseph must have been surprised when this group of strangers showed up at the stable. After the long journey and the birth of the child, the last thing they wanted were visitors! But their surprise turned to awe as the shepherds told their story and worshiped the baby. If we as Christians were more vulnerable at times, we might find more doors of opportunity for witness opened to us.

Question 9. You might encourage members of the group to keep a spiritual journal in which they record the blessings of God and expressions of their own faith and commitment to the Lord. Another approach might be to write a song or paint a picture that recalls a particular blessing or instance of divine care.

Question 11. As a follow-up you may want to ask, "What specific steps can you take this week to begin to tell someone about Christ?"

Study 5. The Day After Christmas. Luke 2:21-40.

Purpose: To explore the positive influence other godly people may have on our lives and futures, and the influence we have on others.

Question 2. The Old Testament Law placed three requirements on Mary and Joseph when Jesus was born. First, on the eighth day after his birth, Jesus was to be circumcised (Lev 12:3). Circumcision was the sign of being part of God's covenant people, Israel. Circumcision was usually done in the parents' home and was also the occasion when the child was officially named.

Between verse 21 and verse 22 of Luke 2 another thirty-three days elapse. Forty days after the birth of a male child, the mother was to offer two sacrifices at the temple for her purification (Lev 12:1-8). Because blood was involved in the act of giving birth, the mother became ceremonially unclean. The sacrifices restored her ritual purity and also served as a reminder of the curse of sin upon humanity. The Law required a lamb to be offered as a burnt offering and a dove or pigeon as a sin offering. Those too poor to buy or to bring a lamb could offer two doves or two pigeons. Since Mary and Joseph offered two birds, it seems likely that they could not afford a lamb.

After the purification offerings had been made, Mary and Joseph were ready to fulfill their third obligation—the presentation of their firstborn to the Lord. God claimed the firstborn son in each family as his own possession. That son belonged to God to serve him as a priest (Ex 13:2, 12-13). After God selected the family of Aaron to be a perpetual priesthood in Israel, God allowed the other families and clans to redeem their firstborn. The parents came into the temple and gave the child to a priest. They were symbolically giving their son to God. The priest lifted the child before the Lord and pronounced a blessing. The parents then paid the redemption price of five shekels and redeemed the child from the obligation of serving in the temple (Num 18:15-16). As the parents received the child back from the priest, they recognized in a fresh way that God's own possession had been entrusted to them.

It is possible that Simeon was the priest assigned that day to bless the sons brought for redemption. More likely, he was simply a godly man who by divine insight recognized Jesus as God's promised Redeemer.

Jesus (through his parents) kept the Law of God even in his earliest years. By his own testimony he did not come to abolish God's Law but to fulfill it (Mt 5:17).

Question 4. Mary and Joseph were setting the example of obedience and honor to God even when Jesus was a baby. Parents cannot begin early enough to model their commitment to the Lord in the ordering of the priorities in their home and in the obedience of their lives to God's Word.

Question 5. Luke borrows a phrase used throughout the Old Testament to refer to a special anointing or empowering of the Holy Spirit upon chosen individuals ("the Holy Spirit was upon him," v. 25). The Spirit's anointing on Simeon resulted in supernatural knowledge. Simeon was waiting for the "consolation of Israel" or the comfort the Messiah would bring, and God revealed that Simeon would not die until he saw the Messiah. The Spirit's anointing brought divine guidance as Simeon was led by the Spirit to come to the temple on a particular day. Simeon also experienced the Spirit's insight as he approached Mary and Joseph and knew that their child was the promised one. The final work of the Spirit was to give Simeon prophetic utterance as he spoke about Jesus' future and Jesus' influence on human history and human destiny.

Question 7. Anna is called a prophetess as were other women in Scripture, for example, Miriam (Ex 15:20); Deborah (Judg 4:4); Huldah (2 Kings 22:14); and Philip's daughters (Acts 21:9). Anna probably overheard Simeon's prophecy and stepped up to confirm his words as a second witness from God.

Question 9. Try to get group members to focus on one or two positive ways that they want to have influence as they grow older. Simeon's righteous life and Anna's godly example were not produced overnight. Their spiritual influence came at the price of a track record of holy living.

Study 6. Spiritual Mentoring. Luke 2:41-52.

Purpose: To grasp the important balance between godly influence and the individual's spiritual growth in the spiritual nurture of children and others.

Question 3. The Old Testament commanded Jewish men to come to Jerusalem for three festivals: Passover (early spring), Pentecost (summer) and Tabernacles (autumn) (Ex 23:14-17; Deut 16:16). Because the Jews had been widely scattered by this time in history, the custom was to come to Jerusalem for only one of the feasts. Jews living near Jerusalem preferred Passover; Jews further away preferred Pentecost because sea travel was safer in summer than it was in early spring. Each year Joseph and Mary came to Jerusalem at least at Passover (a remembrance festival recalling the miraculous deliverance of the people of Israel from Egypt [Ex 12:1-36]) and perhaps for the other feasts. They were devoted followers of the Lord God of Israel.

If Joseph and Mary traveled from Galilee around the area of Samaria, the journey was about an eighty-mile trip. Pilgrims usually traveled in large caravans for protection from bandits and for the fellowship with family members. The normal pace was about twenty miles a day, requiring four days.

We aren't told if this was Jesus' first trip to Jerusalem since infancy, but a boy's twelfth year marked the beginning of an intensive year of study and preparation to assume responsibility for keeping God's Law at age thirteen. The custom of bar mitzvah, which Jews observe today, began long after Jesus' day. Luke's picture of Mary and Joseph taking young Jesus on the Passover journey is designed to impress us with the importance of faithful parents instructing their children in the truths of Scripture. Mary and Joseph modeled their obedience to God.

Question 4. Mary and Joseph probably assumed that Jesus was with relatives traveling in the same caravan. It was only when the caravan stopped and families gathered at night that they realized Jesus was not with them.

Question 5. Mary clearly uses the language of complaint. Her words leave no doubt that Jesus had deeply troubled his parents by his seemingly insensitive actions. They had searched for him with great anxiety and mental anguish.

Joseph and Mary find Jesus in the temple area, sitting with the teachers of Judaism. The customary form of instruction in Judaism was for pupils to enter into question-and-answer dialogue with their teachers. This is the only time in the Gospels where Jesus is said to take instruction from the religious teachers of Israel. Jesus is portrayed as a boy with a thirst to understand spiritual things. While Jesus is listening and learning, he also shows remarkable insight. People were amazed at the answers he gave to the instructive questions asked by the teachers.

Question 6. These are the first words spoken by Jesus recorded in the New Testament. His statement reveals his own set of priorities and a growing sense of his task in the world. Jesus reminds his parents that it is imperative that he should be involved in the process of learning about the Father. He also implies that they should have known where to look for him. Jesus' reference to "*my* Father" shows his awareness of a special and intimate relationship with the Father.

Some Bible students think Jesus' reply was a rebuke to Mary and Joseph for their misplaced priorities. Most students see the statement more as a declaration of his mission. Mary's remembrance and recollection of Jesus' words (v. 51) indicate that she did not see his response as a rebuke even though it exposed her ignorance of Jesus' mission. His words were instead a window into his soul.

Question 7. The Old Testament temple was marked out as the place where God visibly dwelt among his people. In the New Testament age, God's temple is the individual Christian (1 Cor 6:19) and the assembly of worshiping believers (1 Cor 3:16; Eph 2:21-22). Present-day church buildings are not the Father's house in the same sense that the temple was, but there is value in viewing our coming together to worship as entrance into God's immediate presence. *He* is the audience the worshiping church is seeking to please.

Question 8. Jesus' self-awareness of who he was may have come from several sources. Mary and Joseph undoubtedly told him about the visitations and declarations surrounding his birth. As he studied the Old Testament Scriptures, he must have come upon many prophecies that confirmed to him his place in God's kingdom. The inner witness of the Spirit and his growing fellowship with the Father also gave him insight into who he was and what he had come to do. Remember that Jesus was not God pretending to be human but that he was fully human and so had to grow in his knowledge, even in his knowledge of who he really was.

Question 9. Mary and Joseph seem to struggle with the exact nature of Jesus' mission in spite of all they had been told by God. The disciples of Jesus later had the same struggle. They saw all that Jesus did and heard all that he said and still failed to comprehend even fractionally who he was or what his priorities were.

Question 12. If your group is made up of parents, then you may want to cast this question toward parenting responsibilities.

Study 7. Letting Go. John 2:1-11.

Purpose: To show the process of giving up power and authority in someone's life.

Question 1. If you think time will allow, ask what it would have been like if that change had not been made.

Question 3. This wedding took place just a short distance from Nazareth, the hometown of Jesus and Mary. Perhaps this was the wedding of one of Jesus' relatives. Mary seems to have the job of hostess. She was responsible to see that the wedding feast went smoothly.

The wedding feast in first-century Palestine lasted from two to seven days. The bride's family was responsible to feed and care for the invited guests the entire time. If they ran out of food or wine during the feast, it was considered a very serious insult to the guests and a mark of shame to the family. What Mary expected Jesus to do in this situation is unclear, except that she knew he could do something to help.

After the incident in the temple when Jesus was twelve, Joseph is never referred to again as a person who was present or involved in the affairs of Jesus or Mary. Probably Joseph died at some point in the intervening years. Jesus, as the eldest son, would have been responsible to care for his mother.

Question 4. It does seem that Jesus was gently rebuking Mary. Jesus was thirty (Lk 3:23); he had started his ministry; he had already chosen some of his closest followers. Jesus was no longer under Mary's authority, but Mary had not made the transition yet. When the Father would say to Jesus, "Your time has come," Jesus would obey.

If there is confusion about this point, you may want to provide the following comment and question: "Several Bible teachers believe that Mary at first was instructing Jesus to do something about the situation and that Jesus' response was a gentle rebuke to Mary to remind her that he was no longer under her authority. How would you evaluate that conclusion?"

Question 5. Mary is expressing her confidence in Jesus: "Do whatever he tells you." This may be an indication of her growing understanding of Jesus' mission.

Question 6. The family provided large waterpots to be used during the feast for the ritual washing of hands. Archaeologists believe that these pots held twenty to thirty gallons of water each. In order to make wine, two things are needed—grapes and time. Jesus had neither. In an instant of time by his creative word, he brought gallons of wine into existence—and it wasn't just any wine. It was choice wine (v. 10)!

The miracle was the first of Jesus' wondrous works. It was designed (as all his miracles were) to display his glory as God's Messiah and to awaken faith in those who witnessed it.

Question 9. Apparently Mary understood that Jesus was now living fully in submission to the Father. Except for a couple of attempts at intervention in Jesus' ministry, she plays a very small part in the public career of Jesus.

Study 8. Family and Faith. Mark 3:13-21, 31-35.

Purpose: To examine the relationship between our human family and their desires and the lordship of Christ in our lives.

Question 2. Mark writes his Gospel in the nonstop action of our video age. Jesus rushes to do the Father's will. Mark emphasizes the constant pressure of the crowds and the willingness of Jesus to set aside normal human needs in order to minister to hurting people.

Question 6. The relationship of these "brothers" to Jesus has been widely debated. The Roman Catholic Church teaches the perpetual virginity of Mary and explains that these brothers are either (1) cousins to Jesus, (2) Joseph's sons by a previous marriage or (3) sons of another Mary. The most natural reading of the text, however, suggests that they were sons of Joseph and Mary who were born after Jesus. Four brothers are named in Mark 6:3—James, Joseph, Judas and Simon—and sisters are mentioned as well.

Jesus' brothers did not believe in him until after his resurrection (Jn 7:5; Acts 1:14; 1 Cor 15:7), but later became leaders in the early church. It is likely that two New Testament books—James and Jude (Judas)— were written by two of Jesus' half-brothers. The statement in Matthew 1:25 that Joseph had no union with Mary until Jesus was born does not require Mary's perpetual virginity but virginity only until Jesus' birth. There is no biblical reason why Mary and Joseph could not have had a normal marital relationship after that event.

Question 8. Jesus clearly declares and demonstrates that the will and direction of God are to have first priority in our lives. We are responsible to honor our parents (Mt 15:4), but devotion to Christ takes precedence over all other human ties. Jesus said on several occasions that devotion to him would at times produce division even within families, but the genuine disciple would choose Jesus over anyone else (Mt 10:34-39; Lk 12:52-53; 14:26).

Question 9. The family ties that may be broken because of a person's loyalty to Christ will be restored and expanded within the family of believers (Mt 19:29; Mk 10:29-30). Christians have a responsibility to care for and nurture each other as close family members.

If time allows, you might follow up by asking: "How should a Christian relate to family members who are not believers in Christ?"

Question 10. It had been more than thirty years since Mary had heard the startling declarations about who her son would be. The rising opposition to Jesus' ministry from the religious establishment and the reports of his overwhelming work prompted Mary to try to persuade Jesus to take some time off. Even a mother's best intentions have to be weighed against God's purpose and call.

Question 12. Unfortunately, many times family ties are severed or damaged by misunderstanding what it mean to follow Christ. Parents or spouses have been threatened by the zeal of the new Christian. Sometimes Christians have neglected to sit down and calmly explain their faith or commitment to other family members. This question is designed to prompt the members of your group to take one practical, well-planned step toward reconciliation or witness. Even those in the group who have believing families can use this opportunity to express the depth of their commitment to Jesus as Lord.

Study 9. Standing Near the Cross. John 19:23-30.

Purpose: To look at Jesus' tender care for Mary as a model for our ministry to others who are suffering.

Question 2. Four women came near Jesus' cross as he died (in sharp contrast to the four soldiers who callously gambled for his clothes). The other Gospel writers state that several women witnessed the scene from further away (Mt 27:55-56; Mk 15:40; Lk 23:49). The torture and suffering a person experienced during crucifixion must have pierced Mary's heart to its depth.

Question 3. In the middle of excruciating physical and spiritual anguish, Jesus still took upon himself the responsibility of making provision for his mother's care.

Question 6. "The disciple whom he loved" was most likely John, the author of this Gospel. Apparently he was the only disciple courageous enough to come near the cross with the women. It is probable that Mary's sister mentioned in verse 25 was Salome, wife of Zebedee and mother of John (Mk 15:40). John then was Jesus' cousin and Mary's nephew. This relationship makes Jesus' assignment of Mary's care to John even more understandable. Beyond the human relationship, however, John as a member of the believing community was more closely linked to Mary as another believer than were her own sons who were still unbelievers (see Mk 3:34-35).

Question 8. Crucifixion was one of the cruelest methods of execution ever devised by human beings. It was designed to produce maximum agony over the longest time. Yet the cross for Jesus was a triumph.

He finished the work of redemption and by his own willful decision dismissed his spirit. Jesus was not the victim but the victor!

Question 10. If you have people in your group who have not believed in Jesus, this question provides a good opportunity for a presentation of the gospel message. The death of Jesus on the cross paid the price for sin that God demanded and satisfied that demand forever. In ourselves we can never meet the holy standards of God nor could we even pay for our own sin. But someone else has taken the penalty that we deserved and has suffered the full blow of God's judgment. When we personally receive Christ by faith, our penalty is laid on him and his right standing before God is given to us.

Study 10. Our Spiritual Legacy. Acts 1:12-14; 2:1-4.

Purpose: To consider Mary's spiritual legacy and to contemplate our own impact for Christ.

Question 1. The responses to this question could take the entire study time. You may want to ask for one or two volunteers to share their answers. Another approach would be to divide the group into pairs and have them share their responses with each other. Or each person could respond regarding just one of the relationship areas.

Question 3. Jesus' brothers did not believe in him during the years of his ministry (Jn 7:5). After his resurrection, Jesus appeared to James (1 Cor 15:7; this is most likely a reference to Jesus' brother, James), and through James's testimony the other brothers came to believe in Jesus as Savior and Lord (Acts 1:14).

Question 4. Mary's understanding of who Jesus was and of what he had accomplished would have deepened as a result of Jesus' resurrection and postresurrection teaching, just like the disciples' understanding changed dramatically. Mary obviously told the believers about Jesus' conception and early life. Her godly wisdom and servant attitude made her a powerful model in the newly born church.

Question 7. Jesus had promised an outpouring of power (Acts 1:8), but these events must have been startling and energizing to those first followers of Christ. A new day in God's program was dawning!

Question 8. An expectation of God's power will not necessarily reveal itself in a repetition of the events of Acts 2. Unfortunately, many Christians gather for worship without any thought that God may want to break in upon them with a demonstration of his power and grace. We have lost the sense of anticipation that God will do anything new in our worship or in our lives. A change of attitude in our hearts and minds toward what God is able to do might transform our personal and corporate worship into what it is supposed to be—contact with the living God!

Question 11. A legacy takes a lifetime to establish. Even the youngest members of your study group need to take the long view of what impact their decisions will have on others.

Douglas and Karen Connelly live in Flushing, Michigan, with their three children, Kimberly, Kevin and Kyle. Doug is pastor of Cross Church, and Karen is a Bible teacher. Doug is also the author of the LifeGuide®Bible Studies Angels, Meeting the Spirit, Daniel *and* John, *and the books* Angels Around Us, After Life *and* Miracles.

What Should We Study Next?

A good place to start your study of Scripture would be with a book study. Many groups begin with a Gospel such as *Mark* (22 studies by Jim Hoover) or *John* (26 studies by Douglas Connelly). These guides are divided into two parts so that if 22 or 26 weeks seems like too much to do at once, the group can feel free to do half and take a break with another topic. Later you might want to come back to it. You might prefer to try a shorter letter. *Philippians* (9 studies by Donald Baker), *Ephesians* (13 studies by Andrew T. and Phyllis J. Le Peau) and *1 & 2 Timothy and Titus* (12 studies by Pete Sommer) are good options. If you want to vary your reading with an Old Testament book, consider *Ecclesiastes* (12 studies by Bill and Teresa Syrios) for a challenging and exciting study.

There are a number of interesting topical LifeGuide studies as well. Here are some options for filling three or four quarters of a year:

Basic Discipleship

Christian Beliefs, 12 studies by Stephen D. Eyre
Christian Character, 12 studies by Andrea Sterk & Peter Scazzero
Christian Disciplines, 12 studies by Andrea Sterk & Peter Scazzero
Evangelism, 12 studies by Rebecca Pippert & Ruth Siemens

Building Community

Christian Community, 12 studies by Rob Suggs
Fruit of the Spirit, 9 studies by Hazel Offner
Spiritual Gifts, 12 studies by Charles & Anne Hummel

Character Studies

New Testament Characters, 12 studies by Carolyn Nystrom
Old Testament Characters, 12 studies by Peter Scazzero
Old Testament Kings, 12 studies by Carolyn Nystrom
Women of the Old Testament, 12 studies by Gladys Hunt

The Trinity

Meeting God, 12 studies by J. I. Packer
Meeting Jesus, 13 studies by Leighton Ford
Meeting the Spirit, 12 studies by Douglas Connelly